T0114649

Nanna God

L O I S   W I L S O N

BALBOA.PRESS
A DIVISION OF HAY HOUSE

Balboa Press books may be ordered through booksellers or by contacting:

Balboa Press
A Division of Hay House
1663 Liberty Drive
Bloomington, IN 47403
www.balboapress.com
844-682-1282

Interior Image Credit: Drew Willard

Print information available on the last page.

ISBN: 979-8-7652-2782-4 (sc)
ISBN: 979-8-7652-2784-8 (hc)
ISBN: 979-8-7652-2783-1 (e)

Library of Congress Control Number: 2022907516

Balboa Press rev. date: 04/19/2022

CONTENTS

For my grandchildren, with love.

INTRODUCTION

Welcome, Dear Reader, to the world of *Nanna God!*

Nanna God evolved from my deepest belief that God is love... *unconditional* love...and the realization that the way I love my own grandchildren comes closest to being an example of that kind of love.

In a world where the idea of God has been presented for millennia as masculine, warlike, angry and punishing, isn't it (past) time for another way? *Nanna God* is another way.

I want you to know that it is 100 percent okay if you find yourself wondering why you're here right now, holding this book in your hands. Maybe you don't even believe in God! *No problem.* Because I happen to know that this book didn't come to you by accident. Bathed in love and prayer from the first page to the last, it is my heartfelt desire that *Nanna God* will find Her way to precisely the people who need Her most. So here we are.

You may choose to read *Nanna God* however you want. It was written to give you an opportunity to walk with your Nanna for a month, or thirty consecutive days. Imagine a whole month spent with your beloved Nanna, away from the pressures and responsibilities of your day to day a life. A month sleeping in Nanna's house, hearing her humming as she does her daily work, and eating at her table. How refreshing that would be! If that appeals to you, wonderful! I encourage you to spend that time with Nanna in the pages of this book. Or you may want to begin with the chapters that interest you most…reading more slowly or more quickly as you feel led. There is no "wrong" way.

Reading *Nanna God* is a journey. Here are a few supports in case you hit a bump in the road. First, you may not have had a loving, all-inclusive Nanna. If that is the case, then please think of that one special person who has loved you like that, and imagine them as *your* Nanna God. Second, you may have had a Nanna that did not have the means to feed you physical food. In that case, how did she nourish you? With stories? Music? Kisses? Wisdom? Love? Even when Nannas cannot put food in our mouths, they put it in our hearts. Finally, we live in a world where many of us are familiar with masculine language for God. In *Nanna God* we imagine and name God in feminine terms. This is surprising to many people, and can be a welcome change. I am inviting you to open yourself up to this language, which I hope will help you experience the possibility of God's love in new ways.

You will find that each chapter concludes with a little prayer and a sentence for further reflection and journaling. My hope is that you will find these small offerings helpful in leading your deeper into the heart of your Nanna God.

May this book be a blessing to your heart! And know that I am sending you gratitude and love, and prayers for your own soul's unique journey.

It's just what Nannas do.

Love,

Lois

ONE

Nannas Go by Many Names

There are words for Nanna in every language and in every family: Grandma, Granny, Nonna, Bubbe, Grand'Mere, Abuela, Mimi, Mom-Mom... What do you call your Nanna? God goes by many, many names.

I don't think it matters to God one bit what you call God. It could be Allah. It could be Shakti. It could be Great Spirit, Divine Beloved, Adonai. It could be Holy Mother or Higher Power. It could be anything at all. God goes by many, many names.

And just like the many names for Nanna, each one is precious and beautiful.

I have six grandchildren, and they all call me Nanna.

I was their Nanna before they called me anything at all. Before they could speak, before they recognized me, before they knew how much I love them…before all that, I was their Nanna… knowing them, loving them, welcoming them, holding them, comforting them, rocking them. Before they knew me, I knew them. Before they could call me Nanna, I knew their name.

Nanna God is just like that.

And when my grandchildren call my name, I come running with a smile on my face. My little granddaughter Lily is two years old. When she calls out, "Na! Na-na! Na-na-na-na-na!" I come running! I come running to pick her up, to hold her, to see what she needs, to comfort her. With a smile on my face, I come running. It's just what Nannas do.

When you call out to Nanna God, She comes running. She comes running with a smile on Her face. To love you, to hold you, to help you, to comfort you. Not reluctantly, or begrudgingly, not rolling Her eyes, thinking, "Ugh! What do they need now?" No. There is an endless supply of loving and helping when it comes to Nanna God.

So today I want you to think about that. Your Nanna God… She goes by many names. She was busy loving you before you ever knew Her. And when you call Her name, She comes running with a smile on Her face.

Prayer: Thank You, Nanna God, that You come running with a smile when I call. Please help me to trust Your love.

Reflection: What do I call my Nanna God? What does She call me?

TWO

Nanna God has a Long History of Loving

I want to tell you something about myself as a Nanna. By the time I had grandchildren, I had a long history of loving. A *long* history of loving.

I loved my parents and my grandparents, my two sisters, my many friends, my cousins...*lots* of people. Then I loved the man that I married...and then, I loved my children. In fact, my children taught me how to love in a way that I could not have imagined before I had them. And as a mother, that learning went on for decades before the first grandbaby arrived.

Nannas have a long history of loving. By the time our grandchildren grow up, we're pretty darn good at it. In fact, a lot of the rough edges have been worn off. Have you noticed that? Nannas love their grandchildren in way that's a *little bit different* than the way they love their children. It's true. I was stricter with my own kids…and to be honest, less patient. Then my grandchildren came along and I found myself loving them with a patience and the ability to accept them for who they are, where they are, as they are *all day long.*

In other words, I love my grandkids with a lot less ego. It's about them. It's not about me.

So, if Nanna God loves us that way, what does that mean? It means that Nanna God welcomes you and loves you without an agenda for how it makes Her look. She is not one bit concerned about Her image. She loves you for *you*…and it's all about you. And truthfully, there's more patience and permissiveness in Her love than you might imagine.

If you happen to have an image of God that is quick to punish and slow to give you a scoop of ice cream with extra sprinkles, you might want to rethink that image of God. You might just want to consider that maybe your Nanna God thinks it's okay that you want ice cream with extra sprinkles, that you already *have* permission, and that punishment is honestly not on her mind. Because Nanna God has a long history of loving.

Prayer: Thank You, Nanna God, that you are more patient and permissive than I realize! Help me to relax into Your spacious, understanding love.

Reflection: What does it mean to me that Nanna God accepts and loves me exactly as I am? What changes when I see God in that way?

THREE

It Doesn't Matter to Nanna God how You Came Into the Family

I would like to let you know that my grandchildren have come into the family a couple of different ways. I have six grandchildren at the moment, and four of them were born into the family because my kids had kids. Two of my grandchildren came into the family through marriage. They're not biologically my grandchildren, but I love them just as much as if they were. Some grandchildren come into the family through adoption. There are all different ways to come into a family. But one thing is certain: No matter how you come in, you are family now… and you will be loved. It's just what Nannas do.

Here's another thing that is important to know about Nannas. It doesn't matter to them how their grandchildren come in the door. What I mean by that is moment by moment, no matter how my grandchildren happen to show up, they're gonna be loved just as they are. They might come in the door clean, dressed, smelling good and in a good mood...and I am going to love them. They might come in the door in a dirty diaper, wet, crying, cranky, and in a bad mood...and I am going to love them. It doesn't matter how they show up. They're my grandchild and I adore them.

Nanna God loves us all just like that. It does not matter how you came into the family, and it does not matter how you show up at the door. You may have a long history of practicing religion, or you might not. You might have been thinking about Nanna God and loving Her your whole life, or you might have just begun to explore the idea a few minutes ago that there *might* be a God who just *might* love you. It doesn't matter to Nanna God how you show up in the family. The minute you do, she's loving you. And she's not comparing you to anybody else.

Not only that, moment by moment, it doesn't matter how you show up. You might be cranky. You might be full of doubt. You might be full of fear. You might even be angry when you come in the door. Nanna God loves you. She loves you however you show up. She's just glad you're there. That's just how Nannas are.

Prayer: Thank You, Nanna God, that it doesn't matter to You how I came into the family, or how I show up at the door! Help me to always "come as I am" because You love me exactly as I am.

Reflection: How did I come into the family? How am I showing up at the door today?

FOUR

Nanna God Doesn't Waste Anything

I want to tell you something about Nannas: We don't waste anything. We don't waste *anything*. We save stuff, we recycle stuff, we repurpose stuff...we don't waste anything. For example, we don't throw food out. No, no, no, no, no! We scrape leftover food into little containers. And even those little containers are repurposed! They once held something else! They had cream cheese in them, or cottage cheese, or jelly or hummus. We saved those containers. We washed them. We organized them in a cupboard, along with their lids. And now we are scraping leftovers into those leftover containers. We don't waste anything.

We stack them up in our refrigerator and then when the time comes a few days later, we pull them out and we make something new out of something old. We make stew. Or we put it all in a casserole dish and sprinkle cheese on top and pop it in the oven. We make something fresh and delicious out of all the little bits and pieces, all the little leftovers. Nannas...we don't waste anything. We know what to do with all those little raggedy scraps of stuff that appear, by themselves, as though they don't have much value. But when you put it all together... now we can do something *good* with that.

So, I want you to think for a minute about your life. Which, if it's anything like my life (or anybody else's life) is probably made up of bits and pieces and raggedy scraps. And some of them are not so good. Some of them full of pain, some of them full of heartache, some of them are full of mistakes and things you wish you had done differently, if only you had known. My life is like that too.

I want to suggest to you today that Nanna God *loves* to take all that stuff and put it together. She *loves* to create something new and delicious out of those bits and pieces, out of those leftovers, out of those so-called mistakes and bad decisions. When Nanna God looks at you, She doesn't see regret, She doesn't see mistakes, She doesn't see what you should have done. She gathers it all together and She makes a *gorgeous* new thing. She sprinkles cheese on top, and pops it in the oven.

Nanna God doesn't waste anything. She does not waste your tears. She does not waste your heartache. She does not waste the longings that you have that are not fulfilled. She doesn't waste anything. She gathers those things and she blends them together with meaning, and wisdom, and purpose, and love. In fact, Nanna God invites you to hand all that stuff over. Clean out the fridge! Look way in the back! Get out *all* the little containers and put them on the counter. Open them up. Let Nanna God take a look. *Dare Her* to make something delicious out of the bits and the pieces of your life.

Prayer: Thank You, Nanna God, that You don't waste anything, and that You are able to make something beautiful out of all the bits and pieces of my life.

Reflection: What "bits and pieces" would I like to offer to Nanna God today?

FIVE

Nanna God has Perspective

Today I want to let you in on a little secret about Nannas. We have *perspective*. By perspective, I mean that Nannas see things a little differently than other people do. Why is that? Well, frankly, it's because we've been around a while. By very definition, Nannas have been here for a minute. We're not in our twenties, we're not in our thirties, we're usually not in our forties…we've been around five, six, seven, eight, nine decades or so. And that gives us *perspective*.

Things that seem to be an absolute disaster in your twenties look really different in your sixties. Things that cause worry and fear and panic in your thirties and even in your forties look a lot less scary in your eighties. Nannas have perspective. We haven't just lived a long time; we've lived *through* a lot of stuff.

And we've made it through the dark forest to the other side. We're still here.

Nannas have perspective. We don't scare easily. Oh, we've *been* scared! We know what it means to feel fear. We just don't scare so easily *any more*. We have perspective. And that means, when you come to your Nanna with a problem, a worry, a fear, a concern, something that you just can't figure out...something that wakes you up and keeps you up in the middle of the night...when you come to your Nanna with *those* things...not only does she understand, she's not frightened like you are. She's not worried like you are. She can give her perspective to you. And *that* is a gift.

Nanna God loves when you bring those things to Her. Those worries, those fears, those things that keep you up at night. She loves it...because She loves *you*. She doesn't want you to be awake at night worrying about stuff. She wants you to talk to Her about it, and then to listen to Her perspective. Nanna God *always* has something to say. And so, I'm wondering today, what are the things that you can bring to Nanna God? Those things that are worrying you, those things that are puzzling you... what can you bring to Nanna God today? Share it. Share it *all*. Nanna God listens without judging. And then, after you've shared those things with Nanna God...take a deep breath and listen. Let Nanna God share Her perspective with you.

Prayer: Thank You, Nanna God, for Your perspective. Help me to see the things that worry me through Your eyes.

Reflection: What fears and worries can I bring to Nanna God today? What is Her perspective?

SIX

Nanna God Knows How to Do Things from Scratch

Here's something that I know about Nannas: Nanna's know how to do things from scratch. We know how to bake cookies from scratch. We know how to make gravy from scratch. We know how to refinish a piece of old furniture from scratch. We know how to do it. We know how to do it because we've been doing stuff for a long time. And we've had to figure things out.

You see, Nannas have been around longer than Google. We've been around longer than YouTube. We had to figure things out before the answers were right there at our fingertips. And we've been doing it for a long time. Nannas know how to do things from scratch, which means that when *you* are doing something from scratch, your Nanna can probably help you. First of all, she might know something about what it is that you're trying to do. Like roast a turkey or plant a garden. She might know *exactly* how to do it. In fact, if you call your Nanna, you're likely to get a better answer…and a quicker one…than YouTube. Nanna might already know how.

The other thing is that if Nanna *doesn't* know how to do the thing, she's a really good problem solver. This is because she's solved *so many* other problems. So even if she *doesn't* know how to do the thing, she might be able to help you figure it out. Nannas know how to do things from scratch so that they can help *you* learn how to do things from scratch.

All of us, every day, are living our lives from scratch. I've never lived this day before and neither have you. We are making it up as we go along. We are flying by the seat of our pants. Nanna God is *not* flying by the seat of Her pants. Nanna God made the world from scratch. Nanna God made *you* from scratch. And your life (and mine) does not puzzle Her. It doesn't worry Her. It doesn't keep Her up at night.

I'm living my life from scratch today and so are you. Nanna God has some answers. Nanna God has some encouragement. Nanna God has some courage and some strength to give us every day when we wake up and start all over again, living life from scratch. Nanna God loves it when we come to Her and say, *"You know, I've never lived today before. Can You help me? Can You walk with me? Can You give me some wisdom? Can You give me some courage when I need it? Can You help me see the humor in things?"*

Nanna God *loves* to walk with us day by day, helping us live our beautiful, unique, messy lives…from scratch.

Prayer: Thank You, Nanna God, that you love to help me live my beautiful, unique, messy life. Help me remember that I can call on You today and every day.

Reflection: How do I feel knowing that Nanna God is able to help me live my life from scratch today? What does Nanna God have to say to me today?

SEVEN

Nannas Can Make Things Whole Again

Here's something I know about Nannas: We can make things whole again. Nannas know how to put things back together that are in pieces. We know how to make broken things whole.

I love books. One of my specialties as a Nanna is making broken books whole. Books that have been torn by a toddler. Books that have been chewed by a dog. Books that have their covers falling off. A little tape, a little glue, a little time, a little care, a little attention, a little love….and that book is whole again.

Nannas know how to make other things whole as well. Socks with holes. Sweaters with pulls. Dolls that have lost their limbs. In Nanna's hands these things are loved back to wholeness. They are not broken forever. They are not useless or destined for the trash. They only need attention and love.

Nannas know that the most important thing that broken things need is someone to look at them as though they are not broken. To see them as whole, as restored and full of purpose. To know they have not yet finished serving their purpose. Nanna God sees *you* this way.

Perhaps you have been told that you are broken, even broken beyond repair. Perhaps you believe that you no longer have a purpose, that you are worn out and of no use. But Nanna God knows better. She looks at you and sees that you only need a little time, a little care, a little attention, a little love....and you will be whole again.

Nannas derive great satisfaction in restoring wholeness. So does Nanna God. She knows that you are irreplaceable. That you are worth restoring. That a little time spent in Her hands is all you need...and you will be better than new.

Prayer: Thank You, Nanna God, that You see me as though I am not broken. I welcome Your healing love that touches my broken places and makes me whole.

Reflection: What are the broken places I would like to offer to Nanna God today? What does it mean to me to be made whole by Her Love?

EIGHT

Nannas Don't Take Things Personally

Nanna's have been around a while and they've done more than a few interesting things. Because of this, they have been *called* a lot of things...some of them not so nice. We have taken our fair share of criticism and judgement, and we've learned how to let things go. We've learned that not everything that people think and say about us is true. And we've learned how to let that stuff go.

Nanna God knows there's lot of stuff that people say about Her that isn't true. She knows that most people don't understand (yet) how much She loves them. They don't understand that She is on their side. And She doesn't take it personally.

Nanna God wants you to know that whatever you have heard or believed about God until now can be amended. It can be changed. She doesn't take it personally, and She doesn't hold it against you. Nanna God understands that beliefs are like birds that sit in the branches of a tree. With the smallest effort they can be shooed and scattered. It's not that hard to make them fly away.

Nanna God also knows how to help *us* learn how to not take things personally. How to care a whole lot less about the things that people think and say about us. She likes to remind us that folks are probably not thinking about us nearly as much as we think they are! And She likes to teach us how to let go of the things that people *do* say...that we get to decide what sticks and what doesn't.

Most of all, Nanna God loves to help us see ourselves though Her eyes. She knows that that's the real key to not taking things personally. To hold a vision of yourself that doesn't come from the outside but comes from deepest heart of love. When we see ourselves though Nanna God's eyes, all we see is love.

Prayer: Thank You, Nanna God, that You can teach me how to not take things personally. Help me to hold a vision of myself that comes from Your heart of love.

Reflection: How are the judgements of others influencing the way that I see myself today? What does Nanna God have to say about that? How can She help me shift my perspective to align with Hers?

NINE

Nannas Love Growing Things

My Nanna (who I called *Nonna*) loved growing things. In her home she grew African Violets with fuzzy leaves in little white plastic pots near the window. In her yard she grew flowers, grapes, fruits and vegetables. She loved having her hands in the dirt…weeding and watering, tying up tomato vines, pruning wayward shoots and branches. I never knew how much work was involved in gardening because my Nonna loved it so. It never *looked* like work to me, though now I know that it was.

Nannas understand that growing something takes time, and time is something that Nannas understand better that most people. They understand that time isn't something to push up against, because we can't change it no matter how hard we try.

They understand that time is something that we can learn to appreciate…because it has a wisdom of its own.

When a Nanna plants a garden, she knows that each seed will sprout according to its own inner timetable. Some take longer than others. Nannas don't fret over the ones that take a little longer. They know that deep down in the darkness, under the surface, magic is unfolding. They know not to disturb it. To trust the process. To simply let it be.

Nanna God loves us like a seedling. We are Her garden. She knows that we all grow at different rates and in our own time. She understands and celebrates our unique unfolding.

She also tends to us according to our nature. Do we need sun? Shade? Pruning? Watering? She gently stoops and cares for us…but only just enough! She never handles us roughly lest we be bruised or uprooted. "Easy does it" with Nanna God.

Nanna God celebrates *every* aspect of our growth, and *never* compares us to the other growing things in Her garden. Why would She? After all, She knows that each one of us is unique and unfolding in our own time. And She can help us see ourselves…and each other…in this way, too.

Prayer: Thank You, Nanna God, that you tend to me and my growth according to my own timetable. Please help me to be patient with myself and trust the growing process.

Reflection: What are my growing edges right now? How can I be more patient with myself as I grow?

TEN

Nannas Know Who You are and Where You Came From

Nannas know who you are and where you came from. On the day you were born, your Nanna looked at you and saw not only a baby, but also a whole family…a long line of people that stretches back into the past, and a long line of people that stretches forward into the future. The ancestors who loved you into being, and the generations that will come long after you are gone.

Nannas know that people come and people go. They also know that no one is ever *really* gone. Nannas know this because people that they love are gone-yet-not-gone. Their parents and grandparents and great grandparents. People who you may have never met…yet you carry their love and resilience in your blood and in your bones.

Your Nanna looks at you and she sees her father's eyes. Her Mother's quick step. Her Grandmother's tenacity. Her Grandfather's patience. Your Nanna looks at you and also sees the future…descendants that will stretch far beyond her lifetime and yours, carrying the legacy of love that lives in her and now, in you.

Nanna God also knows who you are and where you came from. She knows that you did not arrive willy-nilly on the planet. She knows that you were not a mistake or an accident, no matter what others might say. She knows that you existed in Her Heart of Love long before the day of your birth, and that one day you will return to Her. And that everyone…past and future…will be waiting for you there.

Prayer: Thank You, Nanna God, for knowing me and loving me long before I was born. Thank You that my life is unfolding on purpose and that one day You will welcome me home.

Reflection: What does it mean to me that my life is not a mistake or an accident? What does it mean to me that I came from the heart of Nanna God, and that I will return to Her one day?

ELEVEN

Nannas Tell the Hard Truth

Nannas tell the hard truth. They understand that some things are too important to monkey around. They have learned a lot of things the hard way, and would like to be able to spare you some of those difficult experiences. They see with a clear eye, and they aren't afraid to speak the truth in plain language.

Sometimes we think that love only speaks in soft tones. But this isn't true. Though love doesn't use words to hurt or harm, love can in fact be very direct. Just ask a Nanna who needs to address some foolishness. She will make it plain. *"Pull up those pants! No one wants to see your bare bottom on the train! I know you know better than that!"*

Nanna God also makes it plain. She is never cutting or cruel, but She will get her point across. She has a lot to say to us about all kinds of things: relationships, compromises, boundaries, jobs, commitments…. and She will speak to us by any means She can. She speaks deep down in our intuition. She speaks though the people and things all around us. And if we listen, we can spare ourselves a great deal of trouble and embarrassment.

We never need to be afraid of what Nanna God has to say. We can open our inner ear and *really* listen. And after we do, She knows that we may or may not follow through. She understands that we are free to follow Her advice or let it go. And either way She will keep right on loving us, no matter what.

Prayer: Thank You, Nanna God, that You have plenty of things to say to me, and plenty of ways to say them. Please open my ears to hear You clearly today!

Reflection: What does Nanna God want to talk to me about today?

TWELVE

Nannas Love Strong

Nannas love strong. In a world where the word "love" is tossed around and can mean many different things, the way that Nannas love can be *trusted*. Here's why: Nannas love for the sake of loving. They are not asking or needing anything from the love they give. They don't give love to get love (or anything else) back. It's loving that makes them happy.

This is why Nannas can love each and every grandchild with a whole heart of love. A Nanna's love is never diminished, no matter how many grandbabies come along. A Nanna's love is *not* like a pie that gets cut into smaller pieces with the birth of each grandbaby. It's like a balloon that expends and grows as each new little one is added to the family. There is always more love to give.

It's just like that with Nanna God. She loves strong. She loves each of us as though there were only one of us! And Her love *holds*. Nanna God doesn't let go because She loves us for Love's sake. There are no conditions upon which Her love would end. There is no "falling out of love" with Nanna God.

This is good news, especially for those of us who have experienced all kinds of fickle, conditional love. In fact, those experiences can make it hard for us to believe that strong, lasting love is real. But it *is* real, and Nanna God takes pleasure in showing us that. Go ahead and put Her to the test! Let Her show you just how strong and lasting love can be.

Prayer: Thank You, Nanna God, that You love every one of us as if there were only one of us. Please show me just how strong and lasting love can be.

Reflection: What does the word "love" mean to me? What kinds of love have I experienced in my life? What does it mean that Nanna God's love for me is strong and lasting?

THIRTEEN

Nannas Know What Matters

Do you feel like you know what really matters in life? Do you feel like that sense of "knowing" comes from a place deep inside of you? Or do you sometimes have an unsettling sense that your values are something that you've absorbed *from the outside,* and you're not really sure if those things matter at all? If you feel that way, you're not alone. We live in a world where there's lot of conflicting (and downright foolish) information about what matters. And we're bombarded by those voices from the outside all the time.

Does having "six pack abs" really matter? How about a job that earns "six figures?" Does being famous matter? Having followers? Owning a home or a business? Does youth matter?

How about beauty? A top-of-the-line education? The newest car, computer or phone?

Sitting here right now you may be thinking, "Well I know better than to put much stock in those material, superficial things." *But do you?* Here's a question that gets to the heart of it: *How do you spend your time?* Because how we spend our time reveals what *really* matters to us…and many of us (if we answer that question honestly) have to admit that we are, in fact, spending a great deal of time on materialistic and superficial pursuits. So… *what really matters?* Nannas can help us answer that.

Nannas know what matters because they have lived long enough to observe what *doesn't*. They have lived long enough to watch beauty fade, money come and go, businesses boom and falter, and fame turn to insignificance or disrepute overnight. They have lived long enough to watch the shiny paint wear off to reveal what's underneath. They know from experience that all that glitters is not gold.

They also know that it's possible to dress things up in spiritual clothes and fool people into following something fake and hollow. In other words, all that glitters is not *God*. They know that given enough time, what's there beneath the surface will *always* be revealed.

Notice how your Nanna spends her time. Remember, that's the truest indication of what you really value. What does she do and why? Follow the breadcrumbs of her example and you'll arrive at a life well-lived.

Nanna God also knows what matters. And She truly understands how distracting shiny things can be. She understands that we often miss the best and most fulfilling things in life simply because we are worn out from chasing the things that *almost* matter. So how can Nanna God help? Well, She loves when we ask Her to *reveal our purpose*. She loves to show us that the clues to what matters most are hidden in plain sight. They are revealed in and through the people and things we love most. Not the superficial, fleeting "highs" in life, but rather that deeper, quieter sense of being on purpose, content and fulfilled.

Nanna God also knows that it's never too late to discover our purpose and devote yourself to it. She knows that everything in your life so far has been preparing you for your mission, and that you are right on time. And She knows that once you begin to devote yourself to your purpose, more clues will follow, more doors will open, and a deeper, more lasting sense of happiness is inevitable.

Prayer: Thank You, Nanna God, that You know my purpose. Please reveal what is hidden in plain sight!

Reflection: What are some clues to my purpose that Nanna God has been revealing recently?

FOURTEEN

Nannas Love Diversity

If Nannas have a brand, it's diversity. They are not wedded to just one thing. In the scope of her lifetime, your Nanna has loved *many* things. She has dressed many ways, cooked (and eaten) many kinds of meals, and lived many different lifestyles. Along the way she has kept bits and pieces of it all. Look in her closet. Look around in her home. That hand crocheted poncho is hanging comfortably next to a gown she wore to a special event. That ceramic plate made by her middle child (your Mom) in third grade is on display in the cabinet next to the heirloom china that belonged to *her* Mother. Her life reveals a collection of what she has considered beautiful and valuable to her throughout a lifetime, and it coexists in happy, jumbled, eclectic harmony.

If you were to suggest to your Nanna (and you never would!) that she should just pick one thing, one look, one style and run with it...she would look at you like you were crazy and ask, *"Whatever for?"* Because Nannas know there is beauty in diversity. That loving many things is a hallmark of an open heart and a rich and varied life.

Nanna God loves diversity too. There isn't just one of *anything* on this planet! Even identical twins aren't identical, never mind the fact that no two snowflakes are alike! There is diversity *everywhere*. The idea of narrow categories, binary systems, and only-one-right-way is not Nanna God's style. Whenever you encounter that mindset, you are *not* in Nanna God territory. *I know this for sure.*

And wherever you see wild, abundant, lavish, extravagant, outrageous, eclectic, diversity dancing in exuberant harmony... Nanna God is present, laughing and giving her blessing there.

Prayer: Thank You, Nanna God, that You LOVE diversity! Thank you that you dance over my uniqueness with JOY!

Reflection: How is Nanna God's love of diversity expressed in my life? How does this make me feel?

FIFTEEN

Nannas are Expansive

Nothing rigid can last for very long. That's why Nannas are expansive. They've made it this far because they know how to expand, flex, bend and include. If they didn't, they would have snapped in two a long time ago.

Nannas know that the only way to make it through life is to develop the capacity to allow for change. To not resist the things in life that will inevitably roll in like the tide and rearrange everything...whether we like it or not! Nannas know that *everything changes,* and that we can learn to be okay with that.

And it's not just circumstances that change. Beliefs and values can change too. Nannas understand that sometimes the hardest changes to deal with have to do with changing our mind, our perspective, our point of view. They have experience with rigid thinking and the ways that it can damage relationships… sometimes beyond repair. Nannas value flexibility precisely because they know the damage that rigid thinking, words and actions can do.

Nannas know that all that is required for change to happen is a little bit of willingness and an open mind. In fact, those are two of Nanna God's favorite things: willingness and an open mind.

Willingness is simply saying in your heart that you are open to the *possibility* of something new. That you don't *have to* stay where you are. That *maybe* you'd like to try.

An open mind is simply saying that a new idea is welcome here. That the way you see things might possibly be seen in another way. That there might be many ways…and the door of your mind is open to welcome new thoughts as guests who can come in and sit down and share their way of seeing.

Willingness and an open mind are sisters. They work together to help us expand and grow. And this is why Nanna God loves them so! Because she knows that a whole universe of expansion and growth are right there for us if we invite them in.

Prayer: Thank You, Nanna God, that You can bless me with willingness and an open mind. I ask You for these gifts today.

Reflection: What are some areas where I have been feeling stuck lately? How does Nanna God want to bring willingness and an open mind into my beliefs, circumstances and relationships today?

SIXTEEN

Nannas Don't Quit

Have you ever known a Nanna who was a quitter? Me Neither. Seriously. It's nearly impossible to even *imagine* a Nanna who is a quitter. Nannas by definition are tenacious. They are the ones who keep on going after everyone else has quit. They simply hold on and persevere. Why is that? Nannas know that the breakthrough is just around the corner. They know that right *after* the part that seems impossible, the thing you were working towards finally comes. They have lived this phenomenon so many times that they have *learned to trust it.*

They also know it's not easy. They don't expect you to pretend that the waiting and the struggle isn't hard. They will be honest with you about how tough it is, and they want you to be honest, too. *Just don't give up.*

Nannas have a way of breathing fresh life and hope into the most desperate situations. This is because their fortitude is not pie-in-the-sky wishful thinking. It's based on their own record of resilience. This is why we believe our Nannas when they tell us that things are going to turn out alright.

Nanna God is just like that. She has been in *every* storm. She has walked beside every suffering, scared human who ever lived, and has provided comfort and wisdom and hope when there was nothing but darkness and despair all around. This is Her specialty.

Many people mistakenly think that Nanna God's job is to take the suffering away. They don't understand that suffering is a big part of our curriculum on planet Earth, and that we signed up for it when we arrived here. Nanna God's job isn't to eliminate suffering, it's to *be with us in our suffering*, offering limitless comfort, strength and hope.

Prayer: Thank You, Nanna God, that You are *always* with me in my suffering, offering comfort, strength and hope.

Reflection: Where am I experiencing suffering in my life right now? How do I see Nanna God showing up to walk with me there?

SEVENTEEN

Nannas Tell the Best Stories

Nannas tell the *best* stories. They know so many! They know the story of how we were born. They know stories about when we were a baby. They know the stories of how our parents we born, and what they were like when they were little. They know stories about their own lives growing up, family stories about people you have never met, but who you carry in your blood and bones. They know all kinds of folk stories and stories from books and from history. And they can make up stories where you and your siblings and cousins are the heroes and heroines, deep in a magical forest or a haunted castle, or on a pirate ship.

Nannas understand that stories are powerful. They teach and transform. Stories slip in sideways when our defenses are down and trick us into learning things we might otherwise resist.

Stories also carry memories, the precious remains of people who now walk among us embodied only in photographs and these shared words.

Nannas are the story-keepers, and they know it. That's why they tell the stories they do, so that one day the stories will be remembered and told *after* the Nannas are gone and new Nannas take their place in the long line of Nannas stretching back to the beginning of Time. It is a sacred role. It is holy ground.

Nanna God is a story teller. She is in *all* the stories. She is the fairy who blesses gardens and the jinn who grants wishes. She is the mother rabbit, the tricky coyote, and the resourceful spider. She is the child who sees what the grownups cannot, and the poor old woman gathering sticks. Her voice breathes life into every story, and unites the stories that have been told around fires everywhere, for thousands and thousands of years.

Nanna God understands that each life is a story that we are telling *right now*. She knows that we are the hero of our story, and that we are making it up as we go. She understands that there are villains and helpers and magicians and fools…and that things are not always as they seem.

Nanna God knows that sometimes we are scared by our own story, and that we desperately want to know that somehow it will end well (even when we don't know exactly what that means).

Nanna God understands that sometimes we have a hard time turning pages, closing chapters, and letting some characters go. She understands that our stories collide with other stories, and that some days it's hard to wake up and face the part of the story that we are in right now.

Nanna God especially understands that it takes courage to keep telling your story when you don't know when and how it will end. And She loves you all the more for being *so brave.*

Nanna God is good at helping with the meaning of our stories. She specializes in helping us see the purpose (and even the beauty) in the chapters that are not our favorite. The ones we would tear out if we could. Nanna God asks us to open those chapters up to Her so She can help us create their meaning.

She knows that those sections contain valuable gifts of wisdom, and She wants you to know that you do not have to face them alone.

Prayer: Thank You, Nanna God, that You love and understand my story, including the parts that are not my favorite. Help me to see my story though Your wise and loving eyes.

Reflection: What are some chapters of my story that I can offer to Nanna God for courage? Healing? Wisdom? Strength?

EIGHTEEN

Nannas Love to Sing

Nannas love to sing! They sing while they are doing things, like dishes and laundry and making soup. They sing to help their grandchild stop crying (or whining). They sing to distract us and entertain us and teach us. They sing because it makes them happy and because it makes other people happy too.

Nannas don't care whether or not you want them to sing. They will sing if they want to. They will sing anyway. And they know lots of songs. Funny songs and sad songs and songs that tell stories and teach lessons. They know the *best* songs.

Nannas know that songs can seem to make time go by faster, and they can make hard things seem easier. They understand that when times are tough, a good song can get you through.

Nannas know that songs unite people across time and space and culture and the things that we think divide us. Nannas have sung while marching in the streets for justice for themselves and others. They know the power of voices lifted together in song. They understand that singing is a form of protest and solidarity, and that even after the singers are gone, the song goes on.

Nanna God sings. She sings in the wind and the rain, in the oceans and the rivers, and in the deep night sky. She sings every morning with the birds and every afternoon with the cicadas and every evening with the crickets. Nanna God sang on the day you were born and joined in with your first cry. She sings over you when you are lonely and She sings with you when you are filled with joy.

Nanna God loves your voice. She wants you to not believe whoever told you that you were too loud...or too *anything*. She knows you are exactly, precisely enough, and that when you *lift your voice* in any fashion, your voice pleases her. Whether you sing or write or paint or teach or protest...your voice is precious to Nanna God and She celebrates your every expression. And She wants you to know that She is singing in and with you, always.

Prayer: Thank You, Nanna God, that You love my voice! Help me sing my unique song today and every day without fear!

Reflection: When and where do I hear Nanna God's voice most clearly? How is She encouraging me to lift my voice and sing today?

NINETEEN

Nannas Adore Their Grandchildren

Nannas adore their grandchildren. They are a one-woman fan club. Your Nanna holds every position in the Fan Club of You. She is the president, vice president, secretary and treasurer. She doesn't need any help. Her adoration of you is so deep and wide that the whole club rests on her fandom alone. You are never outside of her adoring gaze.

Nannas don't need one bit of affirmation regarding your wonderfulness. They know that each of their grandchildren is extraordinary, and that is all they need to know. There are no comparisons, either. Each grandchild stands alone in their category, *categorically the best*.

Nanna God adores each of us just like that. The idea of comparing us to one another is absurd to Nanna God. How could you possibly compare two things that are utterly unique? To Nanna God (like our own Nanna) we are, quite literally *incomparable*.

Nanna God wants us to understand this so that we will stop comparing ourselves with others. *Period.* Once and for all. She also wants us to know we have Her permission to stop hanging around people who that to us. Who rate us on a scale of one to ten, who evaluate our beauty, our intelligence, our talent, our worth. Nanna God wants you to know that folks who do that are *clueless,* and they are deeply bruising to the soul. Nanna God says you can walk away. You will not miss them.

Nanna God wants you to know that whenever you need a boost, the door to her Fan Club of You is always open. She also wants you to know that it's okay if you stop by frequently. She is always thrilled to see you.

Prayer: Thank You, Nanna God, that You *never, ever* compare Your grandchildren, and that You can help me learn to appreciate my own *incomparable* worth.

Reflection: In what ways do I compare myself to others? What does Nanna God have to say about that? How can She help me to see myself through Her adoring eyes?

TWENTY

Nannas Feed People

Nannas are excellent cooks, and they love to feed people. For Nannas, food is love. When I was a little girl, there were always good things to eat at my Nonna's house. Homemade pasta, big pots of spaghetti sauce, green beans and tomatoes from the garden, fresh baked bread. There were treats too. Some were homemade, like the dough she tied into a knot and then deep-fried and dusted with powdered sugar. Others were very special store-bought treats, like ginger ale and tiny chocolate wafers with colored sprinkles on top.

When neighbors or cousins knocked at the door, food suddenly appeared on the table...seemingly without effort. The coffee percolator was put on the coal stoves, platters of meat and cheese and homemade pickled vegetables appeared, as well as cookies and anise cake and wine. Everyone pulled up a chair and talked and ate and it was loud (we're Italian) and no one thought of refusing the food any more than they would refuse the laughter or the love.

Nannas feed us because they know the power of sitting around a table and knowing that *you belong*. It is the feeling of home and place and family. And Nannas understand that once you sit down at the table, you *become* part of the family. They insist. There are no strangers at Nanna's table. Only family. There is no them. There is only us.

Nanna God feeds us, and She has a *very* large table. No one is excluded. *No one.* There is always room, always another chair, another coffee cup, another plate of bow tie cookies with powdered sugar on top. So have a seat and try a little of everything. And after that, have a little more. Because Nanna God knows (like all Nanna's do) that you can't rush being around the table together. Time is suspended. Chores can wait. This moment...*this moment right here*, when we are all together...might never come again. It is precious. For all its familiarity, for all its ordinariness, it is also fragile and fleeting. Nannas know this, and so does Nanna God. Here we are, gathered together, belonging...and it is everything. Linger another moment. Have another cookie. *Stay.*

Prayer: Thank You, Nanna God, that at Your table, no one is ever turned away, and everyone belongs.

Reflection: Where have I felt most welcome in my life? Where have I felt most unwelcome? How does Nanna God want to heal those places of unwelcome with Her love? How do those places of welcome serve as an expression of Her love?

TWENTY-ONE

Nannas Know How to Listen

If you really need someone to listen, talk to your Nanna. Nannas are super listeners. That is because they know that in order to have anything worthwhile to say, you have to *listen first*. Nannas listen because they want to understand, and because when they finally speak, they have something worthwhile to say.

It's easy to speak without listening, but it is of little value. We have all had this experience. We know it's true. Nannas have simply reached the point in their lives where they no longer want to use their precious breath speaking words with no impact. There's already enough of that going around.

Nannas also love to listen to our stories because they love us. To receive someone's story is to love them. Every little detail of a grandchild's story is precious to their Nanna. An ordinary

Thursday in middle school complete with a chemistry quiz, tuna salad for lunch and a school play rehearsal is *not* ordinary to your Nanna. It is the stuff of which your life is made, and it is precious to her because you are precious to her. There are no ordinary days because you are not ordinary. To your Nanna, everything matters. It's a glimpse into your heart and soul. And Nanna treats each detail like a nugget of gold.

This is true for Nanna God as well. She loves to hear about your day, your fears, your challenges, your lunch. There is no detail too small (nor problem too large) to hold Her interest. It all matters to Nanna God because *you matter.*

Many people have gotten this wrong. They assume that God is only concerned about "big" problems and "big" solutions. But that's only because they don't understand that God loves us like a Nanna. She knows our favorite kind of jelly and the way we like our sandwich cut. She *cares.*

So, if you find yourself in a situation where what you need most is someone to listen, Nanna God is ready. And She's also ready (if you're willing) to share Her thoughts when you're done. Just a little quiet listening with and open heart is all She needs to find Her way in. And when She speaks, you can count on Her having something worthwhile to say.

Prayer: Thank You, Nanna God, that You care about my life, right down to the details.

Reflection: What does Nanna God want me to share with Her today? What does She have to say?

TWENTY-TWO

Nannas Know That Love is in the Details

When my children were younger and we would visit my parents, my Mother (their adoring Grandma) would have their favorite treats on hand. Slices pepperoni for Josiah, Jell-O salad for Micah and Caleb, cottage cheese with pineapple for Essie. This is because my Mom knew something that all Nannas know well: Love is in the details.

Nannas pay attention. They watch and they listen and they remember. They know your favorite color, your hobbies, your best friend's name and your best (and worst) subject in school. They are interested in everything that has to do with you, and it is catalogued in their mind and heart in a file with your name on it. Because Nannas know that love is in the details.

I learned this from my Mom simply by watching her love her nine grandchildren. As they grew and changed, my Mom continued to learn and catalogue the details of their lives. *And I could see how loved it made each of them feel.* Like a V.I.P. So very special. So worthy. Known and understood and adored.

I believe that every person on the planet longs to feel this way. As though they matter. As though someone cares…truly cares…about the things that make them tick and that make them happy. And I'm sorry to say that *that* kind of love is in short supply. Maybe it's because we are distracted. Maybe it's because we are self-absorbed. Maybe it's because we don't understand how much it matters. But Nannas know, and they *act* on it. And so does Nanna God.

Nanna God knows that love is in the details, and She *acts* on it. She is constantly presenting evidence of this, but don't always notice. You love sunsets? *Look at this one!* You need encouragement? *Here are two text messages and a phone call from three different friends in a single day to lift your spirits.* You want to paint? *Here are your favorite canvases on sale!* Nanna God strikes again.

People often say that they don't believe in God because they can't see Her. But the signs are *everywhere.* And one of Nanna God's favorite requests is, *"Help me see You." Help me see the signs of Your presence and Your love."* In other words, you don't have to whip up faith out of thin air. You can simply ask Nanna God to help you see the ways that *She pours Her love in detailed and specific ways into your life.* And She certainly will.

Prayer: Thank You, Nanna God, for all the ways You reveal Your love to me. Help me to see and recognize the signs of Your presence and Your love.

Reflection: What are some of the special ways that Nanna God reveals Her love to me *in the details?* How can I express my gratitude to Her today?

TWENTY-THREE

Nannas are Soothing

Is there anything in the world more soothing than a Nanna? I don't think so. Nannas are built to be soothing. For one thing, we are soft. In a world where being hard is endorsed, Nannas are the opposite of hard. We are soft. Even a little bit squishy. The parts of us that used to be hard have softened over time, inside and out. Nannas are a soft place to land.

We are also soothing because we don't rush. We used to, but we don't anymore. We have come to understand that rushing can hurt others and ourselves. We have learned that we can often get more accomplished by moving at our own pace and doing one thing at a time rather than all the rushing and "multitasking" we *thought* we had to do when we were younger. Now we simply take our time.

Nannas are soothing because we know that small and simple things can make a difference. A kiss, a hug, a song, a story, a book, a rocking chair, a blanket. These are not fancy remedies. They are not impressive. But they work. And Nannas know it.

Nanna God is soothing like that. She loves to hold us and rock us when we are feeling lonely or frightened or sad. She is always awake in the middle of the night. She is ready at the beginning and at the end of every hard day.

Nanna God loves when we understand that She is a soft place to land, and that the hard, angry "God" that some folks believe in has nothing to do with Her at all. She is, in fact, the Antidote to that whole line of thinking.

So, the next time you find yourself in need of some soothing, climb into Nanna God's lap. She will hold and hum and rock you for a while. Be sure to nestle in extra close, so you can hear the beating of Her Heart.

Prayer: Thank You, Nanna God, that You love to sooth me. Please help me to remember to come to You the next time I need to feel Your tender care.

Reflection: What does it mean to me that Nanna God is soothing? How is this different than the ideas and beliefs about God that I may have carried in the past? What are the ways that Nanna God loves to soothe me now?

TWENTY-FOUR

Nannas Understand Pain

Nannas will do their level best to protect their grandchildren from all kinds of pain. We know that broken bones and broken hearts are equally painful, just in different ways. We honor the pain of a scraped knee and the pain of not getting picked for the team. We understand that all pain deserves to be acknowledged, and that when you live in a small body, small pains are big. Nannas don't rank pain. We honor it *all*.

Nannas have suffered a great deal in our own lives, and we wish we could end all suffering. But we also understand that much of life's pain can't be avoided, no matter how hard we may try. Nannas also know that pain carries its own lessons, and that those lessons are part of living a full and compassionate life.

Nannas will address your pain according to what it is. You hurt your lip? *Here's a popsicle!* You bumped your elbow? *Here's a kiss!* You lost the game? *Here's a hug and a pep talk that will help you believe in yourself again.* You lost a boyfriend? *Here's a hug and a listening ear and some Kleenex for the tears.* Nannas understand that tending to pain is not one size fits all. We also understand that it takes time and attention to do it right. We will drop whatever we are doing and care for the hurt. It's that important.

Nanna God cares deeply about our pain. Many people think that if God loves us, we won't suffer. But the truth is that suffering is simply part of the experience we signed up for when we came to this lovely green planet. We might not remember that we signed up for it, but we did. And that's where Nanna God comes in. She is always leaning towards us, stooping down to hear us when we cry. And She understands that *all* our pain matters...the losses, the loneliness, the heartbreaks and the heartaches, the disappointments, the worries and the fears. There is no pain too small for Nanna God's loving attention.

She is never too busy. She will drop whatever She is doing when we need Her. Nanna God will gather you into Her arms and give you Her full attention every time. She will never mock your pain or call you a crybaby. When you hurt, *She* hurts. She knows your pain is *real*.

One of the greatest changes in our lives can happen when we open our heart to the idea that Nanna God hurts when we hurt, and will ride out the pain we are experiencing *with us*, not as a dispassionate bystander, but as a loving Nanna that will rock us in Her arms until we feel better. It is Nanna's *presence* that makes things better. And Nanna God is always here.

Prayer: Thank You, Nanna God, that You hurt when I hurt, and that my pain always matters to You. Help me to remember that when I am in pain, I can come to You, and You will rock me in Your arms until I feel better.

Reflection: How does understanding that Nanna God hurts when I hurt change my perception of what it means to go through loss, disappointment, loneliness and grief? How does Nanna God want to offer me comfort today?

TWENTY-FIVE

Nannas are Fierce

There is a whole other side to Nannas that at first may not meet the eye. The *fierce* side. Nannas are fierce. For one thing, don't try to hurt my grandchildren. Because there isn't anything I wouldn't do to protect them from harm. Nannas cherish our grandchildren and know that they are *worth* protecting. We will place ourselves in harm's way if it means protecting them from harm.

When I was a little girl growing up in northeastern Pennsylvania, my sisters and I would hike in the forest with my grandparents, foraging for wild edibles. My grandfather (Nonno) always packed a pistol on his belt in case we encountered a rattlesnake. My Nonna always walked with a forked stick. Why? To trap the rattler by the head so my Nonno could shoot it, of course! Yep.

Armed with nothing but a forked stick, my Nonna was going to protect her grandchildren from poisonous snakes. *That's fierce.*

Nannas are fierce in other ways as well. They take no shit. If someone is talking foolishness they will say so. They care not one bit what that person thinks. They will tell them straight up that they are being a fool, and to take that talk somewhere else. And if you try to hurt a grandchild, well… now you have the wrath of a Nanna to contend with, and that is no ordinary wrath.

Nanna God is fierce. She has ways of watching over us and protecting us that we know *nothing* about. She knows that the woods are full of snakes, and she is *prepared.* This is why she urges us to stick close to Her. And why She sometimes tells us that there are some places that just aren't safe for hiking. Especially after dark.

Nanna God's fierce protection sometimes takes the form of things we desperately *want,* but do not *get.* Other times it takes the form of waiting longer than we want to wait. There's a lot that goes into protecting us from harm that only Nanna God knows.

Because Nanna God is fierce, She can teach us about boundaries. She can guide our intuition about who we should… and shouldn't…trust. And because Nanna God is fierce, we do not ever need to seek revenge for a wrong that's been done to us. It's none of our business, and will only serve to make us bitter. Our job is to forgive and move on, knowing that our fierce and loving Nanna God will take care of the rest.

Prayer: Thank You, Nanna God, for Your fierce and steadfast love!

Reflection: What are some ways that I see Nanna God's fierce, protective love at work in my life? What does She want to say to me today about boundaries, trust, forgiveness and moving on?

TWENTY-SIX

Nannas are Creative

Do you need a last-minute Halloween costume? *Nanna can make one out of a paper bag.* Are you missing ingredients that you need for a recipe? *Nanna can tell you what to use instead.* Has it been raining for three days and you are bored and crazy? *Nanna has games and projects that will keep you busy all day.* Nannas are creative. We are brimming with ideas!

Nannas are creative because they have had to solve a lot of problems in their lives, and often they did not have the resources to do it the ordinary way. They had to figure it out and make it work using what they had. And once you do this over and over again, it becomes a habit! Nannas have the *habit* of creativity... and it's a very good habit to have.

The habit of creativity helps you see the *potential* in people and situations. Instead of seeing what you don't have, you see what you *do*. This is why Nannas rarely skip a beat when we come to them and tell them that there's a problem, because they already know that there's a solution. You just need to figure it out.

Nanna God is like that. She is *infinitely* creative. In fact, *all* creativity flows from her! There is no problem that Nanna God can't solve, and often in surprising ways. The same way that your Nanna enjoys a good challenge (*"No eggs for the cake? No problem! We'll use mayonnaise! instead"*), Nanna God enjoys a good challenge. Bring Her anything and everything that is causing you trouble, and soon the solutions will begin to present themselves in the most unusual and surprising ways!

Prayer: Thank You, Nanna God, that You have infinitely creative solutions to *all* my problems. Help me to remember this the next time that encounter a challenge, large or small.

Reflection: When has Nanna God stepped into my life with a creative solution to a problem? What are some challenges I am facing right now where I can ask for Her help?

TWENTY-SEVEN

Nannas are Funny

Nannas are funny. You already know that, right? Your Nanna finds things funny that you don't think are funny at all. That's because Nannas tend to not take themselves...or life...as seriously as they did decades ago. They understand that things that appear to have dire consequences often pan out to be not all that important. They know that there were plenty of things that caused her so much worry and fear years ago...and now they can't even recall the details! They can find the humor in many of life's circumstances because they realize that most things are not actually the emergency they claim to be.

Nannas don't take themselves too seriously. Over the course of our lives we have come to realize that we aren't good at everything, and that's okay. We can laugh at ourselves over what we don't know and what we can't do. We know that other people are good at those things (taxes, for example) and they are happy to help us. We can also laugh at the mistakes we make. We know that our worth is not determined by whether we do things perfectly, and that life is way more enjoyable when we finally stop making the effort to be perfect.

Nannas God is funny, and She is inviting you to lighten up. She wants you to know that the things that you are taking so seriously right now are making you feel heavy, and that many of them are not going to matter five months from now. Nanna God also wants you to understand that injecting a little laughter into life makes everything so much better. It's okay to take a break from all your goals and plans and lists and schedules. Taking time to play clears our mind and lifts our heart and sometimes leads us right to the solution we've been looking for.

If it's hard for you to believe that Nanna God has a riotous sense of humor, look at the animal kingdom. Giraffes look like they were assembled with leftover parts. Orangutans look like a Halloween costume gone wrong. I can imagine Nanna God laughing with delight over every odd and improbable creature, each one quirkier than the next!

If you are having a hard time finding the laughter in your life right now, ask Nanna God to help you. She will be happy to show you how.

Prayer: Thank You, Nanna God, that You care when my life feels heavy. Help me to take a break and find the laughter in my life today.

Reflection: What areas of my life are feeling heavy right now due to my effort to get thing *just right?* How is Nanna God showing me how to take a break and lighten up?

TWENTY-EIGHT

Nannas are Wise

All Nannas teach, all the time. They don't do it on purpose. They are even trying. Nannas teach because they are wise, and they live what they know.

Wisdom doesn't automatically come with age (there are plenty of old fools) though it *is* a contributing factor. However, the other factor is *more* important: the ability to reflect and derive meaning from it all.

Nannas understand that as time passes it's entirely possible to grow older but not wiser. But if you gather your life experiences and pass them through the grid of your own self-awareness, values and purpose...you will, over time, become wise.

Nannas know that wisdom has nothing to do with how smart you are. You can be smart and foolish in much the same way you can be old and foolish. Being smart means you can do a complex math problem or solve a complicated crossword puzzle. But wisdom is much deeper than that, and it doesn't require smartness. It requires careful observation of the world and its people...and observation of yourself.

Nannas are wise teachers, which is why they rarely lecture! They teach by living what they know, and sometimes they use words. It's a lot more fun for the teacher and the student that way...and the lessons sink in deeper, too. Think about your Nanna. What are the things that you have learned from her without even realizing that you were learning? I bet it's a long, long list. And I bet it includes all kinds of things...from how to bake cookies and fold socks to how to always stand up for the truth. Valuable lessons that help you every day...and shaped who you are.

Nanna God is wise. She is the source of *all* wisdom. She holds the understanding of who you are, who we *all* are, why we are here, and what matters most. Tapping in to Nanna God's wisdom will change your whole life. That is no exaggeration. It will put things into perspective, starting with your own inestimable worth. It will re-arrange your life so it makes sense...so that the important pieces get their due attention, and the unimportant pieces are no longer center stage.

Nanna God is always sharing Her wisdom with us...we just aren't necessarily paying attention. There's a lot of noisy competition for our attention these days, and a lot of things that masquerade as wisdom that are actually foolishness dressed up in flashy clothes.

We can recognize Nanna God's wisdom because it isn't flashy. It's quiet and deep and it usually comes to us when we settle down and really listen. And that is something we all can do. Even now, today.

Prayer: Thank You, Nanna God, that You are the source of Wisdom, and that Your Wisdom is *always* available to me. Help me to remember this today and every day.

Reflection: What are the noisy things in my world that distract me and masquerade as wisdom? How can I turn down that noise so I can hear Nanna God's quiet voice of Wisdom? What does She want me to know?

TWENTY-NINE

Nannas Serve with Love

Nannas love to do things for the people they love. When my children were small, we would save all our mending to bring to my Mom (their Grandma). She could work magic with a sewing machine. Hemming, altering, mending…no professional tailor anywhere was as skilled as my Mom. And she didn't do this just for us. She did it for the whole little coal mining town where I grew up. People brought her their jeans and skirts and shirts and jackets. And while they sat and visited with her, my Mom would repair and patch, alter and hem. She never charged a dime. The company was payment enough, along with the joy she derived from being of service, doing what she loved.

My Mom was my lifelong example of humble, loving service. She modeled it for her grandchildren, and for an entire community. When she died, it was her legacy. She loved doing things for the people she loved. Nannas are like that.

Nanna God is like that, too. You are not a bother to Her. She doesn't get tired of you asking for Her help. She loves it, because She loves you. And like my Mom, Nanna God loves the visit. She loves when you sit down to chat while she hems and mends and alters and patches. It's not a fancy visit. It does not require fancy clothes or a fancy building or fancy prayers. Just you and Nanna God, sitting together. And when She's finished you will have your mending done, and you will both be smiling.

Prayer: Thank You, Nanna God, that You love when I sit and visit with You.

Reflection: What are the areas of my life right now that can use a little altering, patching, and hemming? How can I create some time for a visit with Nanna God while she tends to my mending?

THIRTY

Nannas Love Unconditionally

What does it mean to love without condition? It means that there is no criteria, no earning your way into love. It also means that this love cannot be lost...because it wasn't *gained*. It was simply *given*. Nannas love like that.

Your Nanna doesn't love you because she needs you. She doesn't love you because you make her proud. She loves you because you are hers.

Your Nanna loved you as soon as she you knew you existed, which was probably before you were born. Before she knew what you looked like. Before you could do a single thing to earn her love. *That* is unconditional love...and it is rare in this world.

Love like that welcomes us. Love like that heals us. Love like that calls us to be the best version of ourselves, and to forgive ourselves when we're not. Love like that lights up this old world and gives us hope for one more day.

Unconditional love will heal a lifetime of pain. It will dissolve decades of "I'm not good enough." It will bring a blessing wherever it goes, and that blessing is contagious. It is unstoppable.

Unconditional love is never diminished in any way. Disappointment and failure can't touch it. Nor does loss of beauty, strength or wealth. It is unshakable, unalterable, and unsinkable.

Nannas hold this love in their hearts for their grandchildren, and we can **feel** it. It's like bedrock. Truth with a capital T. The law of gravity. Unwavering, certain and strong.

It's so strong, in fact, that it outlasts death. Nannas know this deep, deep down. We know that our love for our grandchildren will outlast our own death, and that when we are no longer here on the earth, we will still be loving them, and they will still be feeling our love. And *that* is the ultimate proof of a Nanna's love.

Nanna God loves *you* like that. She loves us *all* like that. She is the very source of that love, *all* love. It is mine, it is yours. It is our birthright.

There is no earning or losing Nanna God's unconditional, unstoppable love. We don't even have to believe in it! *Because Nanna God believes in you.* Her love is there and it is holding you right now, whether you believe it or not. Nanna God's love beats in your heart and breathes in your breath…and one day it will outlast death as She welcomes you, finally, home.

Prayer: Thank You, Nanna God, for Your unconditional love. Thank You for believing in me. Thank You that You live in my own heart and breath, and that You are always and forever calling me home.

Reflection: When do I feel Love? Wonder? Peace? How do I experience Nanna God in those moments, revealing Herself in my heart, calling my name, leading me home?

EPILOGUE

Your thirty-day journey with *Nanna God* has come to end, but be assured that Her love for you goes on and on. My hope is that now you have become acquainted with *your* Nanna God, you will spend time with Her often. She has much more to say, and looks forward to spending time with you soon.